The Heart Bleeds Over

Georgia Renee Moore

Made with ❤ on the BookLeaf Publishing Platform
www.bookleafpub.in
www.bookleafpub.com

Dedication

To God.
To my family (especially my nieces and nephew, my darlings).
To Mrs. Smith.

Preface

Hello, dear reader! (Do you say "hello" in a preface?)
This is my first published work. It is the work of a 20
year old novice. It is messy and unkempt. It is
embarrassingly vulnerable. It is a dream come true -- at
least, it is to this author, who has been dreaming of being
published for 10+ years!

Some poems in this book deal with topics like self-harm,
suicidal ideation, skin picking disorder, and the general
thoughts and feelings of someone with depression.
Please be sure you are in a safe headspace before
reading!

Acknowledgements

I never would have imagined that a random Instagram
ad would lead to me achieving my dream. I never would
have thought that I would have the courage to take this
leap. I guess all things truly *are* possible through God!

So, thank you to BookLeaf Publishing for creating
#TheWriteAngle writing challenge. Thank you for giving
me this opportunity.

Thank you to my family, as well. From my love of
reading to the photo on the cover, you have made me,
and this book, what it is today. I probably wouldn't have
been brave enough to do this without you. I hope this is
something you can be proud of.

I thank God, most of all. All beauty comes through Him.
He is my Father, Brother, Teacher, Guide, Bridegroom,
Lover, Creator. I pray that His light can shine through
these poems in this book.

Finally, thank you, dear reader, for taking a chance on
my writing! For a poet, I am at a strange loss of words to
express how much it means to me. May God bless you,

and if I don't meet you in this life, I pray I will in the
next!

I. Monster

I want to be a monster.
One that roars and thrashes and terrifies.
I want to devour towns of paper and ink and lead.
I want to be a monster.
A monster that leaves creation in its wake instead of
destruction.

I want to be a monster that brings awe to people.
I want to be an eyesore on bookshelves and walls.
I want my art to be strewn about like blood and
dismembered limbs.

I will be a monster that devours paper and ink and lead.
I will be a monster that makes people's breath catch in
their throats.
I will be a monster that cannot be stopped by any small
means.
I will be a monster that leaves creation in my wake.

II. Mangy Mutt

I have laid at people's feet,
Whining and whimpering,
Looking up at them with puppy-dog eyes.
They have yelled and kicked me to the side.

I have begged for attention,
Even after rejection,
Low-cut tops in their favorite color,
But I am never anyone's lover.

Now I sit in the back pew at church,
So much longing in me to receive you,
But I am dirty,
I am dirty,
I am disgustingly,
Repulsively
Dirty.
I feel I need to tear my skin off to be clean.

God, just let me be clean.

3

III. Bloody Mess

There is blood dripping from my fingertips.
It trailed down my arm from the bleeding heart on my
sleeve.
It is there to be seen,
it won't ever leave.

I've ripped it out,
put it, warm and pulsing, in my mouth,
choked until I've swallowed it down.
Yet still, it returns evermore, to it's post,
no regard for the pain it causes it's host.

I bleed out,
slowly and steadily,
a public execution as I walk down the streets.

I leave blood stains.
On books.
On Blankets.
On beloved people in my life.

I'm so sorry.
I've made *such a mess.*
I'm sorry I can't help to clean it up,
I'm afraid that if I stay I'll make it worse.
Please forgive me.
Please, I beg of you, forgive me.
I've made a mess and I'm terrified to deal with a
consequences.

I think the blood loss is getting to me.

I love and adore you.
I beg you.
Forgive me.

IV. From The Back Deck

I sit outside,
it's the first time in a while.
I got my feet in my seat,
and my stare's a thousand miles.

I hear children's screaming laughter,
and it tugs at my heart.
There are deers in the woods,
it about tears me apart.

V. Evergreen

A peach is rotten to it's pit,
fruit flies swarming all over it.

A doe's heart is being devoured
by vultures on the side of the road.
A car didn't see her when she was trying to go.

Pine needles are falling,
kudzu is choking out the tree.
It's not evergreen anymore.

It's not evergreen anymore
and neither am I.

VI. Like Doubting Thomas, But Worse.

You want to sustain me,
but I eat my own flesh,
convincing myself that self destruction
is self sufficiency.

You watch me,
from up in Heaven,
crash and burn
and crash and burn,
and I'm sure you're sick of it,
just like my parents.

Even babies learn not to get too close to the fire
once they get burned.
I'm dumber than a baby.

Imagine dying for someone just for them to ignore you.
I'm sorry to put you through that.
I'm sorry I stubbornly forge ahead into the abyss,

laser-focused on only what I want.

There's an exhaustion,
bone deep,
that spiderwebs across my body
like the cracks on my phone.
I wonder,
dully,
"why don't you take it away?"

All the answers from faith formations and youth groups
converge in the forefront of my mind,
but hiding in the dark corners are the doubts.
Dark,
sludgy,
rancid doubts.
Doubts I can never seem to fully wash away.
Doubts I can never seem to fully pray away.

I've heard before that doubting leads to deeper faith.
God, let that be true!
Let these tar-like doubts bring me closer to you.

VII. Will There?

Will there ever be a time in my life where I'm not stuck?
Where things flow like the Chattahoochee?
Or will I forever and always be a schmuck?
Just some ape at a typewriter,
waiting for a masterpiece of an accident?

Will there ever be a time when I feel I can breathe?
Air fresh, and clean, and smelling of pine trees?
Or, every chance that I get, will I freeze,
body telling me that I don't deserve that pure air,
lungs seized?

Will there ever be a time where I'm not a baby bird,
throwing myself from high places
in hopes that my wings are finally big enough to fly?
Or will I hit the ground too hard,
broken body forgotten on the forest floor?

VIII. Adult Youngest Child

No one cares about what I'm up to,
they just care a little bit.
They give pity laughs,
and things by halves,
But couldn't give a shit.

I'm the youngest,
I'm the baby,
I'm a child.
I can talk all day but all they'll hear is babble.

I'm not married,
don't have a kid,
don't go to school,
don't play it cool.
What do I do when everyone looks at me like I'm a fool?

Please, oh God,
I just want to someone to talk to.
Please, my God,

I just want a genuine conversation and a smile.
Please, dear God,
I just want them to not to leave me.

This desperation climbs and claws at my throat like bile.
It's embarrassing what I'd do just to have someone stay a
while.

My hands are bloodied,
nails full of dirt,
testament to the lengths I've gone to to climb out of this
hole I'm in.
But every time I gasp for air I still get mud.
I must be deeper than six feet down.

"I'm doing better, I'm doing fine,"
what a bitter and filthy lie.
I talk more and laugh more,
but in the dark privacy of night I still pound at my thigh.
No matter what I do, it's still just me, myself, and I.

Lord, I'm sure this is just a test,
but I guess I don't do well with practical exams.
I feel like an unwelcome guest
whenever I open my mouth.
I feel like I have to be the best
whenever I enter the room,

but that's a futile quest.
That, I'm sure, is true.

I care too much about everything,
or so I've been told,
but I've lived and let go of so many things
and I'm scared of being empty so I hold
and hold
and hold.

God, thy will be done,
but may thy will be gentle,
else I'll burn out like the dying sun.

IX. Imposter Syndrome

Inadequacy is settled deep in my bones,
it's practically marrow, with how deep it goes.
A cannibal could make a high class meal with my
insecurities.

Am I even allowed to write this?
What qualifications do I have?
A high school dropout that read too much.
A poet?
What a joke!
She doesn't even know prose.
You don't have to be good to be published, I suppose.

I'll never be a Shakespeare,
or a Dickinson,
or a Whitman.
I'll forever and always just be a little girl,
too scared to even use her own name.

X. Today Is A Good Day

The air is cool and fresh,
I hear construction down the road.
Today is a good day,
to give God the thanks He's owed.

My cat is laying in sunlight,
and birds are in the air.
Today is a good day.
All God's creatures are fair.

I got up early
and got my errands run.
Today is a good day,
because God is shining His sun.

Family is coming for dinner;
I'll be cooking it soon.
Today is a good day.
God has truly given me a boon.

XI. Prodding, Popping, Picking

Prodding, popping, picking,
My hands move of their own accord,
dancing over skin.

Pus, blood, and scabs
follow swiftly behind fingertips.
Another tissue goes over another wound.

Scratches, scabs, and scars
cover my flesh,
and every day there are new ones,
fresh.

Arms, chest, back,
all a canvas for unwarranted gore.
When did my body and mind go to war?

Prodding, popping, picking.

My mom says I let too many things get under my skin.
Maybe this is just my way of getting them out.

XII. Feeling Better

I'm feeling better,
slowly but surely,
not as under the weather
and I know that God holds me securely.

The next time I feel down,
(which will certainly come soon.)
hopefully I won't feel the want to drown;
I'll just pray and watch a cartoon.

Now, if I feel myself slipping
back into a downward fall,
instead of quitting,
I must simply recall,
that God, with me, is sitting.

And if there is God,
there is love.
And if there is love,
there is hope.

And if there is hope,
there is God.
And if there is God,
there is love.
And if there is love,
there is hope.
And if there is hope,
there is God.
And if there is God,
there is love.
And if there is love,
there is hope.
And if there is hope,
there is God.
And if there is God,
there is love.
And if there is love,
there is hope.
And if there is hope,
there is God.
And if there is God,
there is love.
And if there is love,
there is hope.
And if there is hope,
there is God.

XIII. Heaven Is A Garden

Man came from dirt,
just like the trees.
Adam came first,
then, propagated from his rib, came Eve.

Wind blows through our lungs like it blows through
branches.

Tears drip from chins like dewdrops from leaves.

Veins flow with blood just as rivers flow with water.

Fingerprints spiral on akin to rings in a tree.

The nervous system and mycelium both used electricity
to communicate needs.

Imago Dei were we created,
and though humans were saved best for last,
God made the earth that we live off of in our image.

When I was young
I had a vision
of what I believe is Heaven.
It was a garden.

XIV. Tick Tock

Tick tock,
tick tock.
The procrastinator's biggest enemy is the clock.

I see the finish line
for the race against time,
I'm barrelling straight towards it,
I just need a couple more rhymes.

Twenty-one poems,
Twenty-one days,
it's going by so quickly,
as if I am in a haze.

XV. I'm Sorry

Mommy, I'm so sorry I come to mind whenever you think about suicide.

Daddy, I'm so sorry that you're always cleaning up my messes.

Grandma, I'm so sorry that the shower wasn't loud enough to drown out when I cried until I threw up.

And my brothers and sister, I'm so sorry that I keep making promises I never keep.

And I'm so sorry to God, I keep mistreating the body He so lovingly created.

And I'm so, devastatingly, sorry to myself. I'm sorry I'm never good enough for my own standards.

XVI. Felon

My poems hardly ever rhyme,
and that makes me feel like a felon
even though I know it's not a crime

If it's not perfect
it's a sin.
Every flaw feels like a body-check.

Running behind,
with all the defects in mind,
it feels I'll never make deadline.

XVII. Comparison

Comparison is a losing game for everyone involved.
Either you are pushed to the ground and stomped on
or you are held to suffocatingly high standards.

I have been both.
I have been imprinted into the earth.
I have been stranded where there is no oxygen.

I have compared myself.
Others have compared me.
I have compared others.

Comparison must have come from the apple.
One bite and suddenly everything is competition.
One versus the other.
A perceived "winner."
All losers.

XVIII. Hopeless Romantic

I must have read too much romance,
because now I daydream about unattainable
relationships.

Is it too much to ask for a guy to tell me
that his favorite color is the shade of my eyes?
Or that he thinks of me whenever he smells peaches?

Am I wanting too much when I say that
I want him to make the first move?
When I say I want to be pursued?

Is it too fantastical to imagine a man
who sees me and wants to know more?
Is it too outrageous to imagine him
falling in love with me once he does?

I know I'm young
and that I have plenty of time to find The One,
but I have never had a requited love

and a girl can only take so much rejection.

Is it so absolutely batshit insane to want
a guy that loves my quirks
and colored hair,
my funky fashion
and harebrained hobbies?

Is it unreasonable to want him
to want to have kids?
Or be in love with God?
Or be caring and compassionate?

It feels like I'm certifiable
just for wanting someone to reciprocate
the love I'm always willing to give.

XIX. Sheep In Shepherd's Clothing

I've never wanted to be a leader,
it's never been my aspiration,
always willing to go with other's plans
instead of my own.

But now I've been handed responsibility,
been forced to accept that my life effects other's,
grown a backbone.

I try to give it to God,
lean not on my own understanding,
leave it all at the foot of the throne.

But I'm only human,
always in over my head,
I'm barely even grown.

I'm just a sheep

in shepherd's clothing,
haphazardly sown.

XX. A Letter To Ex Friends

I think I can finally read the book you gave me,
and enjoy all the other gifts too.
They are just objects,
not representations of you.

When it all went south
I gave myself a new hairdo.
Buzz cuts don't suit me,
but it helped me move on from you.

It's been a couple of years,
but thinking of our ending still makes me blue.
I hope you're doing well,
I, for one, feel brand new.

Maybe one day we can be friends again,
once we all have new points of view,
but for now, I am doing well,
and I hope you are too.

XXI. Love Without Sacrifice
Is Cowardice

I'm always so scared of loss.
I hold on to things and loved ones and myself
with a white-knuckled grip.
By the time I realize anything is gone,
all I'm left with is crescent shaped cuts on my palms.

The Father takes my hands in His,
gently,
tenderly,
lovingly.
He pries my fingers away
and kisses it better.

The Holy Spirit leads me
earnestly,
wisely,
lovingly.
They show me the vastness of it all;
the smallness of me.

The Son, my Brother, teaches me,
kindly,
passionately,
lovingly,
that sacrifice is the truest form of care.
He places my hand in His side.

God, grant me the grace to give it all,
give all of myself,
until all that is left is You.